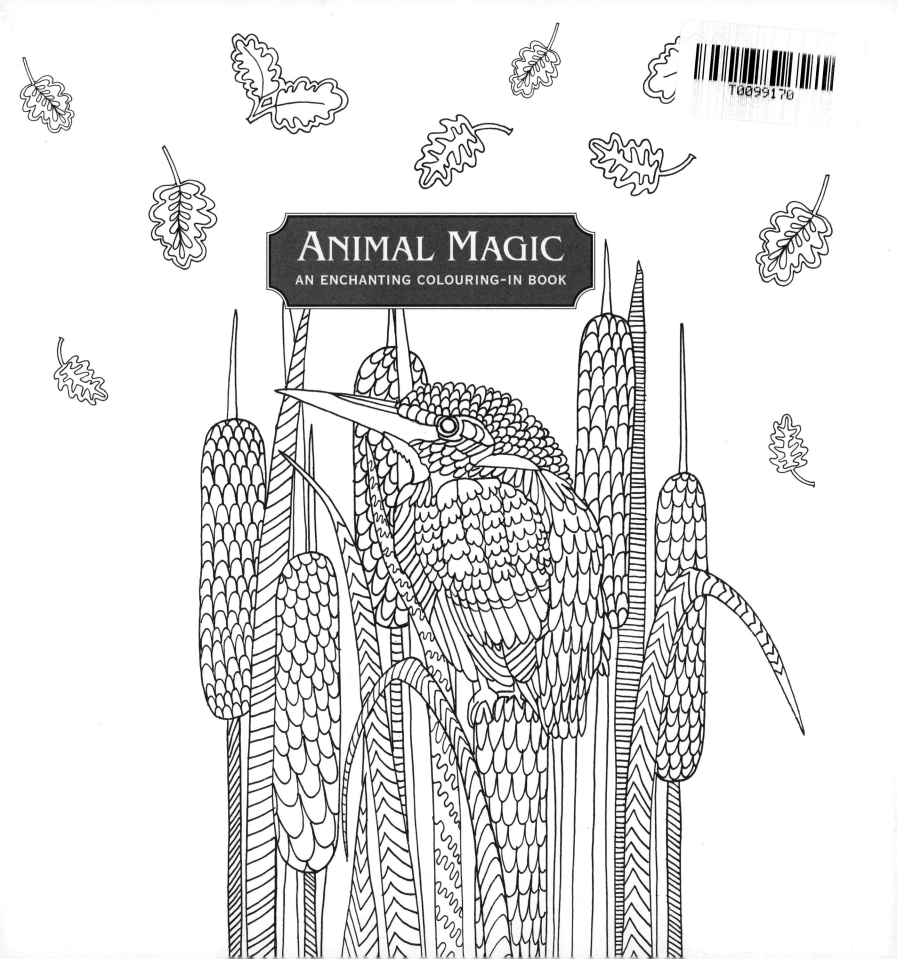

ANIMAL MAGIC

AN ENCHANTING COLOURING-IN BOOK

ANIMAL MAGIC

AN ENCHANTING COLOURING-IN BOOK

· · · · ·

FAY MILADOWSKA

SOUTHWATER

Animals are such agreeable friends –
they ask no questions, they
pass no criticisms.

GEORGE ELIOT

THIS BOOK BELONGS TO

· · · · · · · · · · · · · · · · · · · ·

INTRODUCTION

Our lives are getting busier. Deadlines creep up unexpected, while technology and social media makes it harder to wind down and relax with friends and family. Fortunately, we are now much more aware of the adverse effects of stress upon our lives, and how techniques such as mindfulness can help to alleviate it.

Colouring-in is a form of mindfulness, and it has enjoyed a renaissance amongst all ages, as a way of clearing our minds of distractions, taking some time to ourselves and nurturing a feeling of peace. A classic activity for children, colouring-in appeals equally to adults for its blend of beautiful illustrations and sense of calming satisfaction. At any time in the day it provides a chance to escape the hectic world and discover your inner artist.

In this inspiring book you will find 100 enchanting images of different animals, all waiting to be brought to life with vibrant splashes of colour. Each page offers a fresh delight and you can spend countless hours lost in this magical animal realm, where lions, giraffes and pandas roam alongside iguanas and elephants. In this world there are no rules: start in the middle, return to an earlier work, or design a fanciful mouse.

It is up to you to make these drawings your own, whether you prefer broader strokes of colour or filling in each tiny detail. The act of colouring is a personal experience and a chance to find out which methods work for you to relax and unwind; all you need are some coloured pens or pencils!

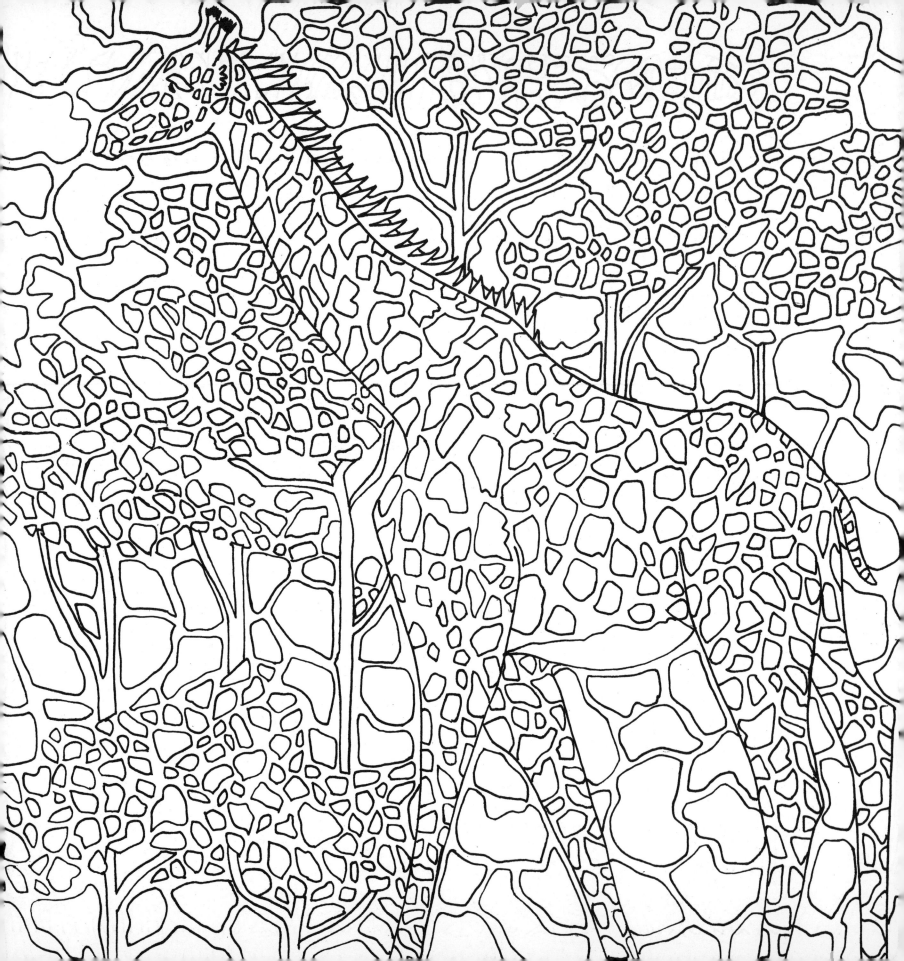

An animal's eyes have
the power to speak
a great language.

MARTIN BUBER

The greatness of a nation and
its moral progress can be
judged by the way its
animals are treated.

MAHATMA GANDHI

A bird does not sing
because it has an answer.
It sings because it has a song.

CHINESE PROVERB

What is life?
It is the flash of a firefly in the night.
It is the breath of a buffalo
in the winter time.
It is the little shadow which runs
across the grass and loses
itself in the sunset.

CROWFOOT

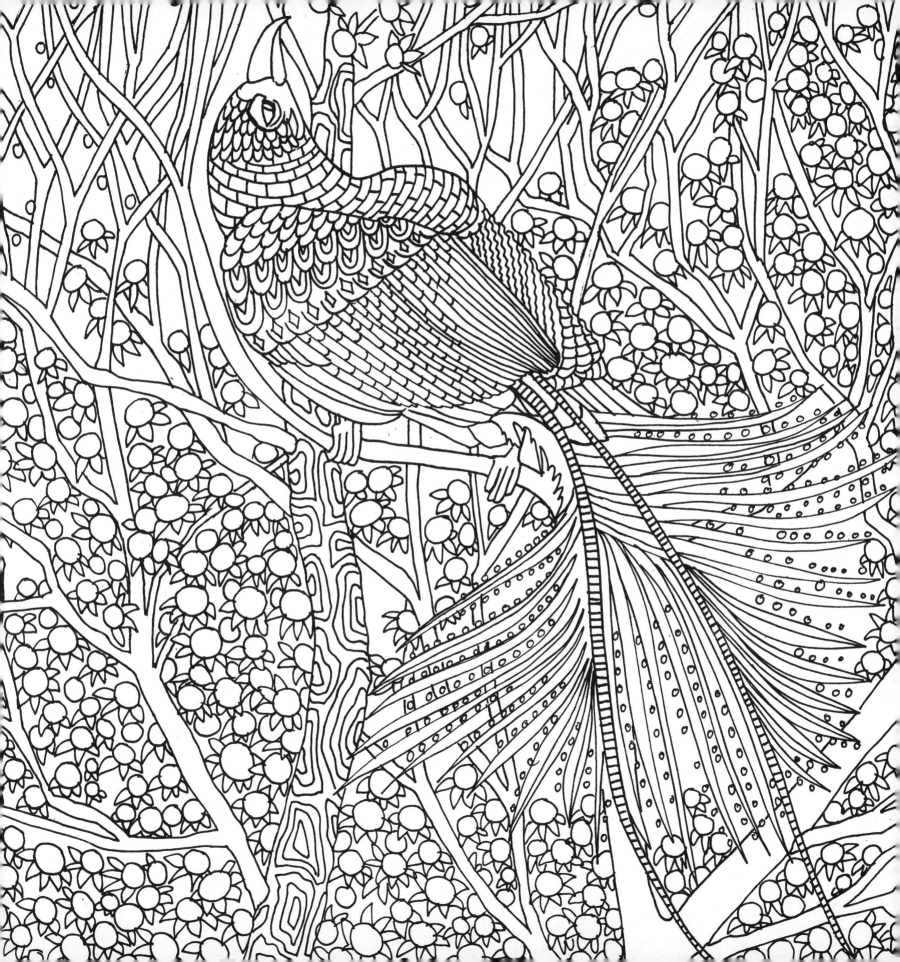

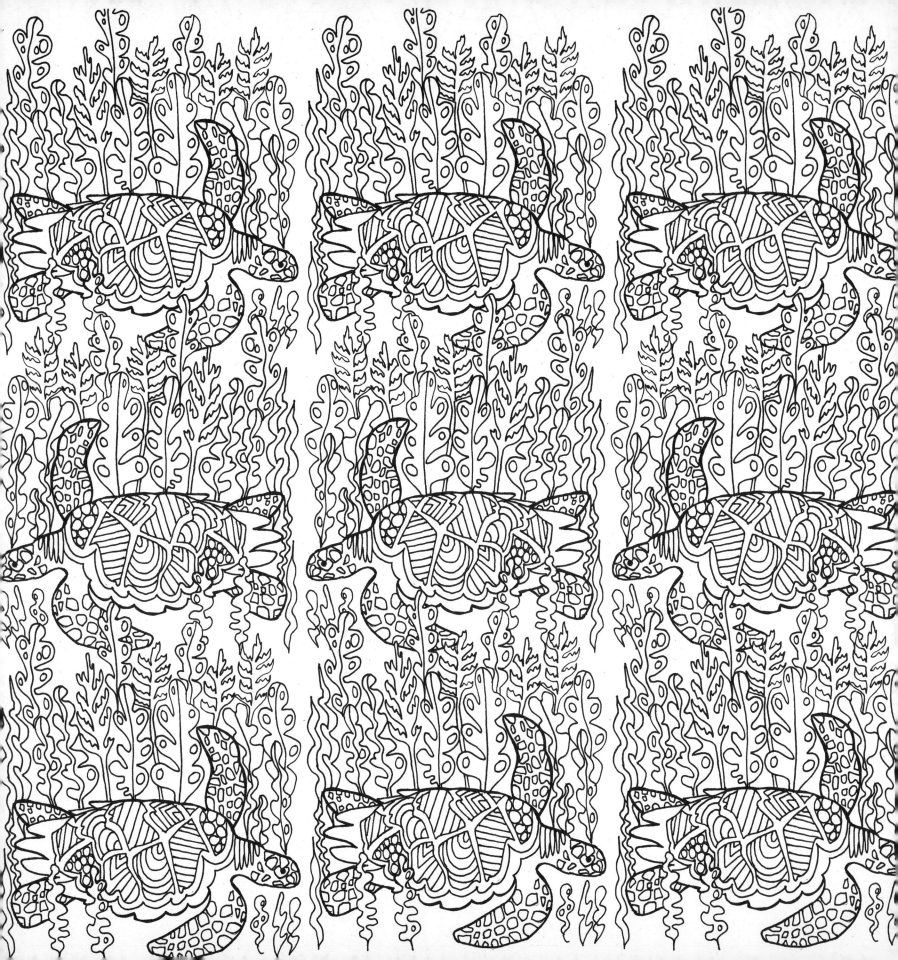

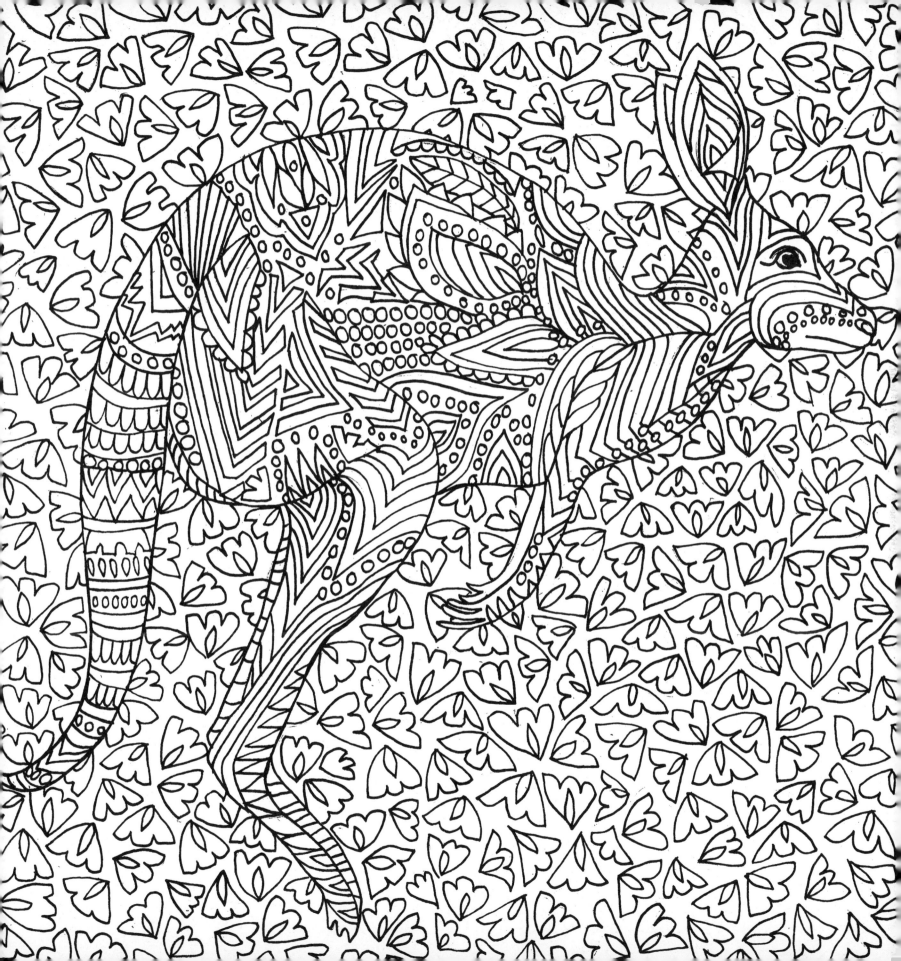

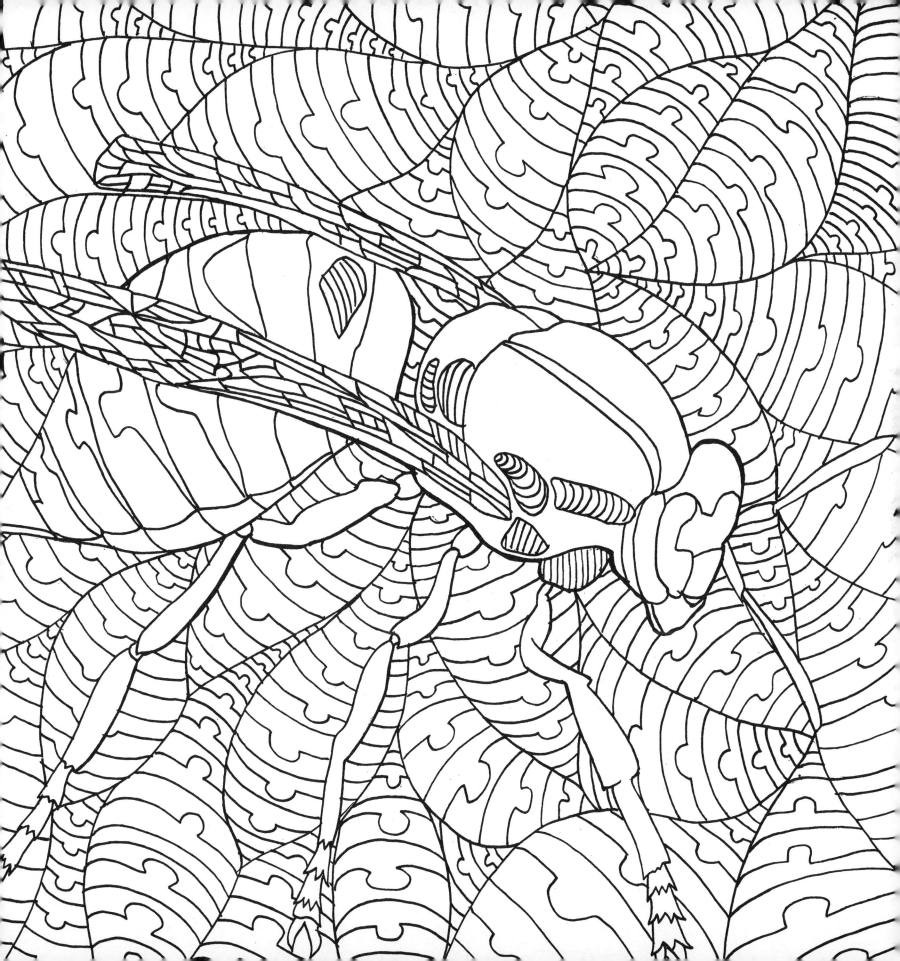

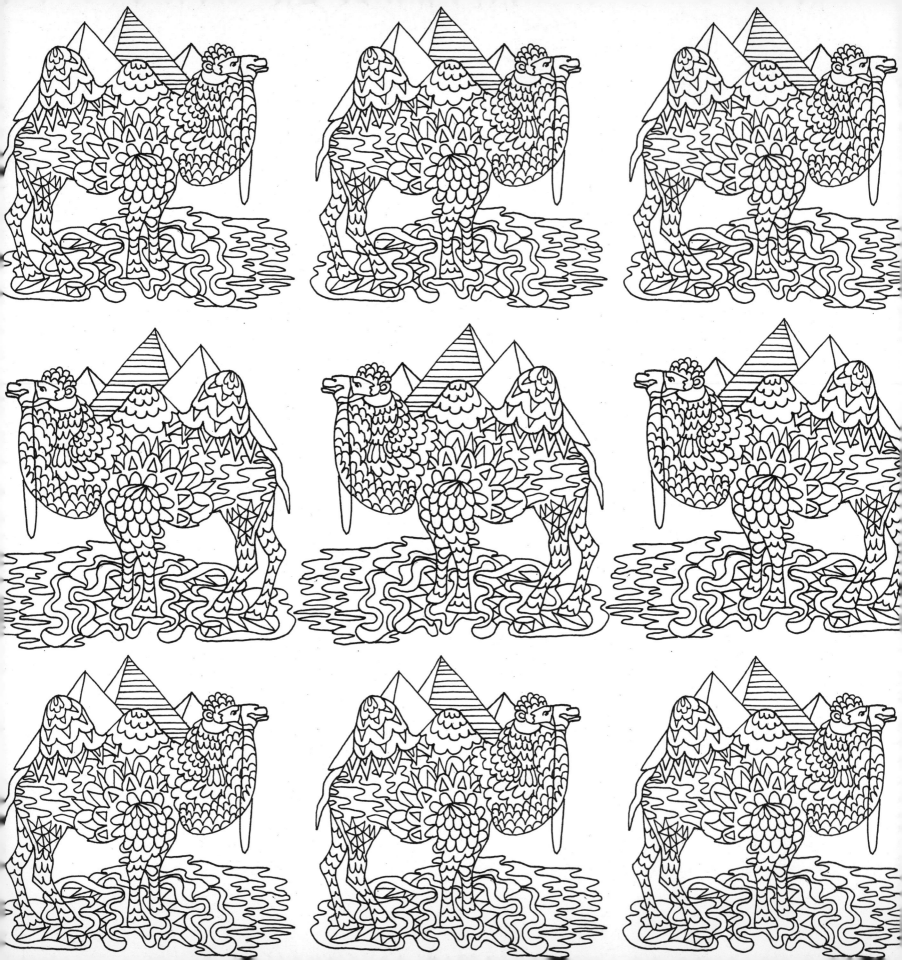

This edition is published by Southwater Books,
an imprint of Anness Publishing Limited,
108 Great Russell Street, London WC1B 3NA
info@anness.com; www.annesspublishing.com
twitter: @Anness_Books

© Anness Publishing Limited 2016

A CIP catalogue record for this book is available
from the British Library.